I know this dream, it might be crazy,
But it's the only one I've got.
(Bob Dylan)

*This story is dedicated to, and in memory of,*
*Elisabeth Javor and Marsha Schneider,*
*two wonderful teachers and human beings.*

# Wendy's Wonderful Window

Illustrated By
**Sandra J. Hoover**

Written By
**Ronald S. Javor**

**W**endy and Mom shared a broken-down place;
The owner fixed nothing, it was a disgrace.
When the toilet stopped working, he wouldn't repair.
So they loaded their bags and they left in despair.

**W**endy packed up her clothes and her coloring book,
And Teddy, her bear and companion, she took.
They loaded the car as the sun went away,
And wondered where they'd go before the next day.

**W**endy woke up and she stretched her small arms.
She heard the birds singing, but no clock alarms.
She looked out her window and what did she see?
Castles and Mickey, and gates for entry.

Wendy tied her shoelaces, and smoothed out her clothes.
Mom braided her hair, weaving rows upon rows.
She stepped out the door with her mother in hand,
And they stared at the wonders—it was Disneyland!
They walked by the park, and saw fresh laughing faces;
This truly was one of the world's happy places.
From outside the fence they saw cartoons they loved,
Some in big masks, and some others white gloved.

The day passed so fast, it was time to sleep tight;
Wendy pulled up her blanket and rested all night.
When Wendy awoke, out the window she looked.
She saw fishermen wading, and fish they had hooked.

**T**hen she opened her window and smelled the salt air,
And gathered her clothes and chose yellow beachwear.
The waves were all roaring, the sand hot and white,
And she played on the beach until late in the night.

After dinner she slept, but her bed seemed to shake;
She dreamed of good food, a potato and steak.
The sun peeked in her window; gold arches were near.
Mom smiled and said, "Want some pancakes, my dear?"

**W**ith Teddy along, they all walked a few blocks,
And stopped at a shop to buy sneakers and socks.
In a market they bought some grape jam for their bread,
And that's what they had for their dinner instead.

As nighttime arrived, Wendy shut all the doors,
And soon all you heard was her breathing and snores.
In her dreams she moved on a wide and fast road,
Between trucks and large lights, she and Teddy they flowed.

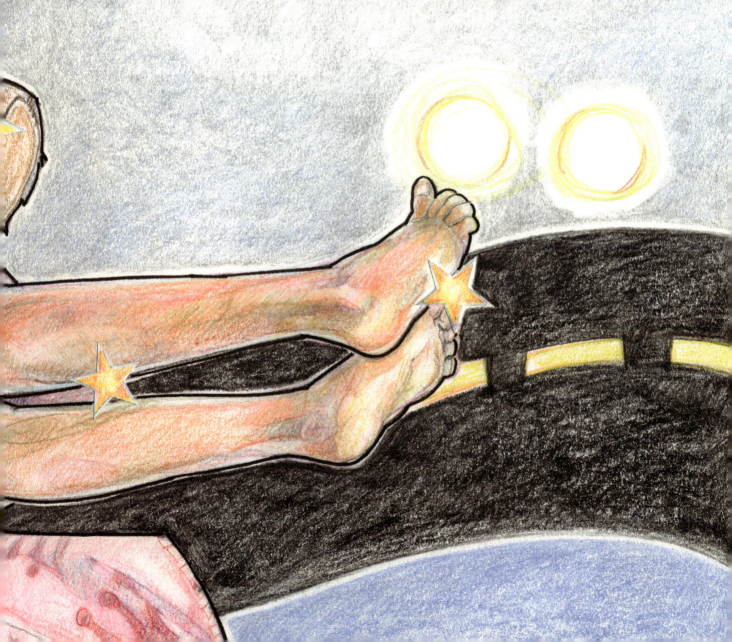

She woke with a start and looked out her window.
A forest was there, the trees row upon row.
Some deer were nearby and a rabbit hopped past,
Several squirrels chased each other, chattering fast.

They walked down a path; on a blanket they lunched.
Their hands were all red from berries they munched.
Wendy napped in the sun and she swam in a river,
And wished someone might come with some pizza to give her.
After some hours, she rested her eyes.
Another day passed, oh how quickly time flies.
Wendy crawled in her seat, Teddy grasped in her arm.
She was happy and tired, and safe from all harm.

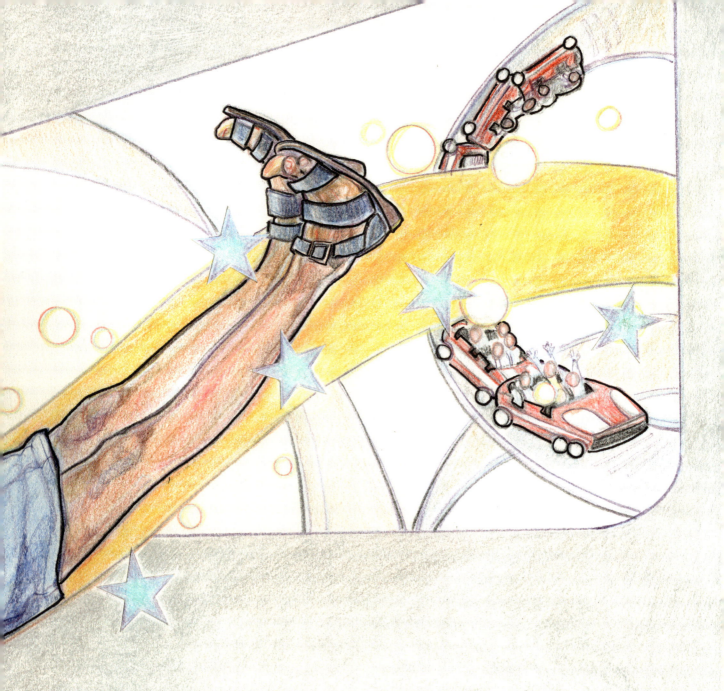

Another surprise came with new morning sun.
Through the window she saw roller coasters and fun.
They couldn't go in, Mother told her, "Alas,"
"I have no more cash, but for food and some gas."

They shared a cold soda, two hot dogs and fries,
And when the gate opened, they heard children's cries.
The coasters they roared, up and down and around.
But Wendy, now sad, merely walked on the ground.

They got into their car and drove to a gas station;
A sink with hot water, a special occasion.
They went back to the beach with its welcoming sand,
And romped and relaxed, their day truly was grand.

**A**t evening they went to their car in the shade,
And PBJ sandwiches carefully made.
They ate dinner quietly, Mom sad, was thinking,
About how they'd live, as their money was shrinking.

The moon soon was up, and a cool breeze arose.
They could hardly stay warm; they had thin summer clothes.
Wendy wished hard on the first twinkling star,
And then fell asleep and dreamed they'd gone far.

At daybreak, an officer knocked on the door;
Through the window he said, "You can't sleep on the shore."
"You should live in a house, with a bed very soon,"
"Instead of on roads and out under the moon."

Now you might guess, Wendy's window's not magic,
She lived in a car; where her life was so tragic.
They moved every night to avoid an arrest,
But compared to a tent, this was really the best.

Wendy and Mom, they were homeless, you see.
They lived in their car because rent, it was free.
But they wished for a house they could live in and sleep,
Where their clothes and belongings they safely could keep.

**W**ith some help from good people, her mom found some work.
No longer outside would they park, eat, and lurk.
Wendy hugged her and kissed her, Mom smiled and said,
"Our lives will be better," and kissed her forehead.
They found a nice house that they could call their home.
And Wendy and Teddy have a room of their own.
The windows have curtains but only one view.
No more adventures, they've started anew.

**In 2013, over 270,000 grade school students
in California were homeless.**
(California Homeless Youth Project)

CPSIA information can be obtained
at www.ICGtesting.com
Printed in the USA
LVIC05n2330141214
418847LV00004B/21